Badges

For A and P

Badges

philip attwood

THE
BRITISH
MUSEUM

Published in 2004 by the British Museum Press
A division of the British Museum Company Ltd
46 Bloomsbury Street, London WC1B 3QQ

ISBN 07141 5014 2

Philip Attwood has asserted his right to be identified as the author of this work.

A catalogue record for this title is available from the British Library.

Designed by Seagulls

All photographs are taken by the British Museum Photography
and Imaging Department and are © Trustees of the British Museum.

acknowledgments

My thanks go especially to all those who have generously donated badges to the British Museum, of which this book illustrates only a small selection. I would also like to thank those colleagues in the Museum who have helped in various ways with this book, and particularly Richard Blurton, Joe Cribb, Renée Friedman, Janet Larkin, James Robinson, Judy Rudoe, Sovati Smith, Christopher Spring, Helen Wang and Dyfri Williams. I also owe a debt of gratitude to various individuals outside the Museum who have answered my queries and provided information and ideas: Anthony Daniels, Richard Doty, Kate Eustace, Tom Fattorini, Polly Gaster, Marshall N. Levin, Joyce Mellor, Robert A. Rush, Rupert Snell and Emily Tarrant. Finally, the book would not have been possible without the hard work of its editor Isabel Andrews, its designer Jonathan Baker, and Stephen Dodd, by whom most of the photographs were taken.

introduction

Badges in Britain; buttons in the United States. The two terms used on different sides of the Atlantic say something about the history and functions of these objects – and also perhaps of the two countries themselves.

Badges exist in the abstract, as in the complaint of Shylock, the Jew of Shakespeare's *The Merchant of Venice*, that 'sufferance is the badge of all our tribe'. They also take many physical forms. During the late Middle Ages the badge was principally a device that identified a lord and indicated loyalty on the part of his followers. The term was also used to define some of the objects on which these devices appeared, an appropriation that implicitly acknowledges that badges are ideas in material form.

The word 'button' has very different associations. Its use in this context derives from a manufacturing process developed in the United States. In the 1890s the New Jersey firm of Whitehead & Hoag, specialists in the manufacture of advertising novelties, began to produce a new sort of button for the adjustable straps that held up men's trousers, in which the cloth was trapped between a circular, flanged piece of metal and a circular metal collar by a simple stamping process. In 1896 this was adapted to make 'all classes of jewelry, such as cuff-buttons, and especially link-buttons, stick-pins, badges [and] brooches', and later the same year the firm announced further 'improvements in badges for use as lapel pins or buttons, or other like uses'. The new badge quickly became the standard twentieth-century type: a protective disc of clear plastic and a paper disc bearing a message positioned between a circular disc of metal and a metal collar, with a sprung steel pin inserted in the back. The similarities with buttons attached to clothing determined the use of the word for badges in America.

These American button badges of the 1890s were, however, by no means the earliest mass-produced wearable objects bearing messages. For around 350 years from the late twelfth century, literally millions of badges were made for Christian pilgrims visiting Europe's holy shrines. These were bought at the shrine itself or in surrounding shops, and (despite the pilfering of badges, as perpetrated by the miller and the pardoner in Chaucer's *Canterbury Tales* and doubtless others) direct sales and shop taxes provided valuable sources of income for the religious authorities. In medieval Britain they were called 'signs'. Originally bright and shiny, they were cast in cheap alloys and fitted with loops, so that they could be stitched to clothing, or a pin. Valued for the talismanic properties that they were believed to derive from their shrine, they also had a more practical appeal in the enhanced status they gave the wearer as a devout Christian. The images that appeared on them were sometimes accompanied by words in the manner of many modern badges. Examples from Amiens read 'Here is a sign of the face of the blessed John the Baptist' (fig. 1).

Secular badges proclaiming the wearer's allegiance to a lord were also in use by the thirteenth century. Those close to a particular magnate might wear one of precious metal, but more lowly individuals would have base metal or cloth badges. The growth of political factions and the sense of invulnerability that a badge gave its wearer could create problems and, in the late fourteenth century, the British parliament tried in vain to limit their use, citing robbery and extortion among the crimes committed by their wearers and noting that 'it is certainly the boldness inspired by their

1

1. *St John the Baptist, pewter badge, France, late 13th or early 14th century*
2. *Edward III and Queen Isabella, pewter badge, England, late 1320s*
3. *John Wilkes, gold badge, UK, about 1763*

badges that makes them unafraid to do these things and more besides.'

Other medieval badges appear to have been satirical in intent. Those showing a boy kneeling before a queen, some of which bear the word 'Mother', are thought to refer to the power exercised over the young Edward III by his mother, Queen Isabella, in the late 1320s (fig. 2). If this is so, these satirical badges also have a political dimension that brings them close to the modern badge. Like other medieval badges satirizing physicians and friars, they use humour to make their point – a tool commonly used in today's badges with equal effectiveness.

In their appearance medieval badges resemble pieces of jewellery, and jewel-like badges have continued to be made into modern times. In eighteenth-century Britain gold badges in support of the champion of free speech, John Wilkes, were formed from the number '45' (it was in the forty-fifth issue of *The North Briton* that Wilkes accused the government of lying) and a band inscribed with the word 'Liberty' (fig. 3). These were the work of gold- and silversmiths. From the late nineteenth century inexpensive enamelled badges, produced largely in

2

Birmingham, became popular. The Primrose League made use of jewel-like badges (p. 22), as did the suffragettes (p. 76), and not dissimilar enamelled badges continue to be produced in large numbers today.

But the development of the medal in Italy from the 1430s and its introduction to other European countries in the sixteenth century provided an alternative, two-sided model for political badges. The medal's juxtaposition of image and text and, from the sixteenth century, its use as a worn object made it an ideal vehicle for political messages. Early examples are the so-called beggars' badges (in Dutch, *Geuzenpenningen* or beggars' medals) that

3

in the 1560s and 1570s those opposed to the inflexible policies of the Spanish government of the Netherlands suspended from ribbons around their necks. This close relationship between badges and medals continued in the following century. The one-sided 'Badges of Silver' worn by some of Charles I's soldiers during the English Civil War were almost certainly of the same design as the front of two-sided medals presented for bravery in battle – the forerunners of today's military decorations. The first British school badges, which came soon after, were also medallic in style. The royal charter of 1672 founding a Mathematical School at London's Christ's Hospital specified that the boys were to wear certain 'Badges and Cognizances upon their Blew Coates'. The die for the badges,

which showed a schoolboy with allegorical figures representing learning, was executed by the medallist John Roettier; like Charles I's military badges, they were one-sided silver pieces with the edges pierced to allow them to be sewn onto clothing. In 1716 another badge was introduced to the school, to be worn by those pupils benefiting from a foundation provided by one of the school governors. On this piece three boys are engaged in counting, writing and weighing, with Latin legends that translate as 'By number, weight and measure. Through the munificence of Henry Stone, Esq.' (fig. 4).

4. *Christ's Hospital Mathematical School, silver badge, UK, 1716*
5. *Wolverhampton Political Union, tin medal, UK, 1831*
6. *The abolition of slavery in British colonies, tin medal, UK, 1834*

4

5

6

Each of the boys is shown wearing the badge itself. The danger of using a precious metal became apparent in 1735 when six of the boys were caught trying to sell their badges.

Base metals were a more usual material. From the early nineteenth century medals were struck cheaply in tin and copper alloy through new, mechanized processes and pierced so that they could be worn. They came to be used as electioneering tools (p. 20), as mouthpieces for causes such as parliamentary reform (fig. 5), and as celebrations of political victories (fig. 6). The subsequent move from the nineteenth-century medal to the twentieth-century badge was directed by the continuing search for ever more economical ways of communicating a message. The button badge of the 1890s came about as the result of developments in various new technologies: the mass-production of aluminium, the invention of celluloid, and advances in colour printing. Its success was due to its cheapness. Whitehead & Hoag stressed that their badges could 'be quickly put together at a minimum expense to the manufacturer and with a great saving of time and labor' and noted the similar appearance of celluloid-covered paper and the more expensive enamel work of conventional badges. In turn, the 1917 American patent for a new production technique pointed out that the button badges made in this way were 'exactly similar in appearance to the ordinary type of paper and celluloid covered metal buttons, but ... produced at an exceedingly less cost'. Under this process, which suited large quantities only, many copies of the image were transferred directly onto a flat sheet of metal; this was then covered with a protective, transparent liquid solution that remained flexible when dry, and the badges were then cut out and shaped mechanically.

There are, of course, many calls for more elaborate badges. Precious metal and intricate workmanship may be used to endow certain badges – and, by extension, their wearers – with a more elevated status, as in the presidential badges commissioned by certain societies (p. 48). Other badges are rendered more expensive by the incorporation of gimmicks, for example, the 1930s' craze for badges backed with a small light bulb connected to a battery carried in the pocket (p. 17) and, more recently, badges containing tiny computers that play a tune (the British Museum's collection has an example from Ronald Reagan's 1984 presidential campaign that plays *The star-spangled banner*). But the vast majority of political badges are made cheaply so that, with as little expenditure as possible, as many as possible can be distributed. In keeping with this general progression towards more economical methods of production, just as the badge replaced the medal, so the self-adhesive sticker is now often more favoured as a vehicle for political messages. Cheap to print, they have the added advantage that they can be fixed to any surface (fig. 7).

The precise form given to a political badge depends on a balance between the requirements of manufacturer, issuer and wearer. Whilst the manufacturer's motivation is usually profit, the issuer seeks to promote a cause, but both are not always equally well served: the rival parliamentary candidates in Yorkshire in 1807 would seem to have gained little from their electioneering medals, but could not risk being without a weapon that was being

---

7. *Self-adhesive stickers issued by the Scottish National Party in support of creating a separate Scottish Parliament and allowing that Parliament to set taxes, UK, 1997*

deployed by their opponents, whereas the manufacturer Edward Thomason did very well (p. 20). The motives of the wearer are more varied, and can include a desire to promote a particular cause, the individual's need to be situated within a group, and a human propensity for self-adornment. Although the ostensible function of a badge is to communicate information to others, the effect it has on the person wearing it is generally of greater significance. Some large-scale issuers may hope that sheer numbers exercise an influence also on non-wearers (and for this a simple design that communicates directly makes the most effective badge), but for most issuers it is the focus that badges give to the wearers' commitment that is important. This is recognized in a Birmingham badge manufacturer's catalogue of 1928, which seeks to impress the point on potential issuers. A group of badges of

different political parties are placed under the heading, 'Nothing keeps Members together better than a nicely made Badge' (fig. 8). The accompanying text explains: 'Enthusiastic members are absolutely necessary for the success of any Political Association. When Members wear Badges they feel they belong to the Association, are members of it, workers for it. Keep them enthusiastic – nothing has been found so successful as the use of Thomas Fattorini Badges, made in the correct party colours.'

Not all badge wearers are this earnest. In John Mortimer's retrospective novel, *Paradise postponed*, the crowd at a 1960s music festival 'seemed to parody the idea of peace. The badges that they wore like campaign medals not only said "Make Love Not War" but "If It Moves, Fondle It", "Down With Pants" and "Position Wanted".' In the early 1980s anyone so inclined could wear a badge produced by London's Badge Shop that satirized three contemporary political causes by uniting them into the amusingly nonsensical slogan, 'Gay whales against

9

racism' (fig. 9). But indications of the importance placed on badges in modern life are numerous. Examples include the regular disputes between employers and their employees over the wearing of badges, the controversy centring on the substitution of white poppies for red by pacifist groups (p. 85), and the long-running debate over the British preserves manufacturer Robertson's use of 'golly' badges to promote its marmalade. First introduced in 1920, the 'golly' came to be regarded by many as a demeaning and racist image, and it went into retirement in 2001.

The resonance of badge designs and slogans is also confirmed by frequent

---

8. *A page from Thomas Fattorini's* Distinctive enamel badges *sales catalogue, UK, 1928*

9. *Gay whales against racism, UK, about 1981*

recycling. The Polish Solidarity logo (p. 42) has been adapted for use by British Unionists in Ireland (fig. 10). The Campaign for Nuclear Disarmament (CND) becomes the 'Campaign for No Defence' in a Conservative Party badge (fig. 11), whilst in another, issued by the Coalition for Peace through Security pressure group, a fist is brought down onto a shattered CND emblem (fig. 12). 'Nuclear power? No thanks' becomes 'Soviet missiles no thanks' (p. 57) or, in the hands of the nuclear industry, 'Nuclear power yes please' (fig. 13). 'Keep [the] GLC working for London' (p. 71) becomes 'Keep the Hayward working for London' in a badge issued by the Arts Council (fig. 14). This response to a Greater London Council plan to take over the running of the Hayward Gallery turns a slogan and design against the very body that had created them. Reaching back over a longer time period, 'I'm backing Britain', a patriotic slogan of the 1960s (fig. 15), becomes in the 1980s 'I'm backing Brixton', a pledge of support for increased investment in this inner London area after the 1981 riots (fig. 16).

Over the centuries issuers of political badges have consistently tried to modify the thoughts and beliefs of individuals. In contrast to these unchanging motives, the appearance of the badges themselves has altered greatly, the result of a succession of technological advances. These advances have ensured that badges have retained their appeal, both for issuers and wearers. But another important factor in the continuing popularity of the political badge has perhaps been a growing, if unproven, belief that 'ordinary' people can help make a difference. These badges are material evidence of this gradual change, as well as a visual record of the crucial events and transitory issues that together constitute history.

10. *Unionist solidarity, UK, about 1987*

11. *Campaign for No Defence, UK, about 1987*

12. *Smash CND, UK, about 1985*

13. *Nuclear power yes please, UK, about 1985*

14. *Keep the Hayward working for London, UK, 1984*

15. *I'm backing Britain, UK, about 1968*

16. *I'm backing Brixton, UK, 1982*

10
UNIONIST
Solidarity

11
CAMPAIGN
NO FOR
DEFENCE

12

13
NUCLEAR POWER
YES PLEASE

14
keep
THE
HAYWARD
Working for London

ARTS COUNCIL

15
I'M BACKING BRITAIN

16
I'm
backing
Brixton

the british monarchy

This two-sided medieval badge, worn as a mark of allegiance to a lord, finds a modern equivalent in badges worn in honour of kings and queens. But whereas a medieval follower expected favours or protection in return and might wear the badge continually, more recent badges have generally been reserved for specific events and signify a very different relationship between monarch and subject.

The Commonwealth (1649-60) saw the production of large numbers of badges in support of the royalist cause. Many portrayed Charles I, executed in 1649, and his family. This heart-shaped silver badge (1) was both a memorial to the dead king and a declaration of the wearer's support for the monarchy.

The accession and coronation of the young queen Victoria saw the beginning of the practice of wearing badges of allegiance at such times, a practice that still continues. Most took the form of pierced medals, but innovative printed badges, glazed and framed and with a loop for suspension, were made by the Birmingham firm, Kettle. This example has a portrait copied from an engraving after a drawing by Sir George Hayter (2). The same etching plate was reused by Kettle the following year for coronation badges, by which point the quality of the image had declined noticeably.

The first coronation to be celebrated by button badges took place in 1902, with the badges imported from the United States. A paper disc inserted into the back of this example (3) indicates that it was distributed by A.P. Jordan, an outfitter in London's East End. Many badges were produced for the anticipated coronation of Edward VIII before the king's abdication in December 1936 made them redundant (4). Manufacturers then rushed to have badges ready for George VI: this example (5 and right) has a miniature light bulb at the back to illuminate the barely recognizable portraits.

---

1. *Charles I memorial, England, about 1649*
2. *Victoria's accession, UK, 1837*
3. *Edward VII and Queen Alexandra's coronation, USA, 1902*
4. *Edward VIII's coronation, UK, 1936*
5. *George VI and Queen Elizabeth's coronation, UK, 1937*

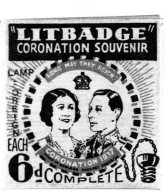

The box for no. 5, UK, 1937

the british monarchy

Badges celebrating the monarchy continued to be produced in large numbers after the Second World War (1) and for all the major royal events of the second half of the twentieth century. The coronation of Elizabeth II in June 1953 (2) brought excitement to a country still experiencing rationing, with over twenty million people – more than half the population – watching the ceremony on television.

The variety of badges produced for the coronation was equalled by those marking the twenty-fifth anniversary of the queen's accession to the throne (3). But the intervening years had seen the rise of the badge as a vehicle for political protest, and in the 1970s republican sentiments – long felt but not previously proclaimed in this way – began to appear on badges. 'Abolish the monarchy' was a favoured slogan, as was 'Stuff the jubilee'. Sherrl Yanowitz, designer of this badge (4), coupled anti-monarchism with a protest against reductions in public services.

The royal wedding of 1981 (5) also saw a range of protest badges. The humorous style of this example (6) conceals a serious message, advising Princess Diana against linking herself with the monarchy. Celebratory badges also appeared for the wedding of Prince Andrew and Sarah Ferguson five years later (7); this particular example was sold at a Trafalgar Square stall on the day of the wedding. Neither of these royal marriages was to last, and the monarchy was to come in for a great deal of criticism in the 1990s. But the large number of people who turned out for the queen's golden jubilee in 2002 suggests that the paucity of badges made for that event was a result of evolving attitudes to the roles of badges rather than to the institution of the monarchy.

1. *Royal visit to South Africa, UK, 1947*
2. *Elizabeth II's coronation, UK, 1953*
3. *Elizabeth II's silver jubilee, UK, 1977*
4. *Stuff the jubilee, UK, 1977*
5. *Prince Charles and Princess Diana, UK, 1981*
6. *Don't do it, Di!, UK, 1981*
7. *The Duke and Duchess of York, UK, 1986*

british politics

The earliest British electioneering badges were made for use in Yorkshire in 1807 and took the form of two-sided medals that were pierced so that they could be worn (1-3). Although at this time only a small minority of men and no women could vote, popular support could greatly help a candidate's chance of success – and these medals were visible signs of popular appeal.

They were made by the enterprising and irrepressible Birmingham manufacturer Edward Thomason, who took advantage of the excitement that resulted from this being the first time that Yorkshire had been contested in sixty-six years. Thomason, who happened to be in Yorkshire when Parliament was dissolved, realized that he had stumbled on a marketing opportunity. Sending word back to Birmingham, he ordered the preparation of steel dies, from which medals for the three candidates could be struck, along with more than twenty thousand pierced tin discs. He must then have consulted with the candidates or their agents because, according to his memoirs, the next day he was able to send notice of the wording that was to appear on the medals. Four days later the dies had been engraved with the various slogans, and the medals had been struck.

At the count fewer than a thousand votes separated the winners, William Wilberforce, the celebrated opponent of slavery, and Lord Milton, from Henry Lascelles, but the operation was so successful from Thomason's point of view that a few days later he mounted a similar exercise in Liverpool, this time making some thirty thousand medals.

---

1. *Wilberforce for ever, UK, 1807*
2. *Milton for ever, UK, 1807*
3. *Lascelles for ever, UK, 1807*

1

2

3

british politics

Photo by]   [Russell & Sons.

LADY PENDER.

Lady Pender wearing Primrose League badges, from The Lady's Realm, *UK, 1902*

Although no women could vote in national elections in Britain until 1918, the number of men allowed to vote was increased enormously by various Parliamentary Reform Acts of the nineteenth century. This development made it increasingly important for the political parties to introduce effective national propaganda machines, which targeted both men and women.

One of the earliest national party political organizations was the Primrose League, formed in 1883 and named after what was said to be the favourite flower of Benjamin Disraeli, the charismatic Conservative politician and former prime minister who had died two years earlier. The League made much use of mass-produced enamel badges, which, being sold to members, helped raise funds. The many varieties of badge reflect the organization's hierarchical nature. This example (1) has the League's motto, 'Imperium et libertas' (Empire and freedom), and monogram, PL, around an enamelled primrose flower.

The importance of the badges as a rallying point is indicated in a verse from a League song quoted in *Lark Rise*, Flora Thompson's book on Oxfordshire village life in the 1880s and '90s:

> *O come, ye Tories, all unite*
> *To bear the Primrose badge with might,*
> *And work and hope and strive and fight*
> *And pray may God defend the right.*

According to Thompson, 'the pretty little enamelled primrose badge, worn as a brooch or lapel ornament, was much in evidence at church on Sundays'. Attractive because of their resemblance to jewellery, they were also effective political statements. A report in *The Lady's Realm* in 1902 (left) called them 'the outward sign and strength of the power of the League and the principles it professes. The sight of the Primrose League badge has in some cases done as much to win recruits as the ablest of addresses and most eloquent of appeals'.

1

---

1. *Primrose League, UK, about 1889*

british politics

The photographic button badge, developed in the United States in the 1890s, was taken up enthusiastically by parliamentary candidates in British elections in the early years of the twentieth century.

This badge (1) shows the Liberal politician David Lloyd George, a Member of Parliament for fifty-five years and prime minister from 1916 to 1922. When Lloyd George first entered Parliament in 1890 as the representative of Caernarvon Borough, he was the youngest member. The badge was probably produced around the time of the 1906 general election.

Other politicians made use of campaigning badges with less success. The Liberal prime minister Henry Asquith called two general elections in 1910. For the first, in January, this badge (2) was issued by Sir Thomas Bramsdon and R.C. Lambert, the Liberal candidates for Portsmouth's two constituencies. Although Bramsdon was the sitting Member of Parliament, the voters decided that on this

1

2

occasion neither man was for them. The Liberal candidates in the ensuing December election, H.D. Harben and E.G. Hemmerde, were equally unsuccessful. Their campaign included some very economical badges, made by coating Bramsdon and Lambert badges with a white background, onto which the letters 'HH' were stencilled in red, but they also produced this elegant badge with their photographs juxtaposed (3). In the same election J.J. Blayney, the Conservative candidate for Clitheroe in Lancashire, also failed to be elected (4), and in 1924 a similar fate befell B.G. Lampard Vachell, Conservative candidate for Wednesbury (5), who lost by only 338 seats.

A later Labour party badge is directed specifically at women (6), who first won the vote in Britain in 1918 and gained equal representation in 1928.

1. *Lloyd George, UK, about 1906*
2. *Bramsdon and Lambert for us, UK, 1910*
3. *Harben and Hemmerde for Portsmouth,*
   UK, 1910
4. *J.J. Blayney, UK, 1910*
5. *Vote for Vachell, UK, 1924*
6. *Vote Labour, UK, about 1935*

british politics

1

2

3

After the Second World War national badges (1) largely replaced local badges for electioneering purposes. The Conservatives were generally the first to find new ways of communicating with the public, using an advertising agency to produce posters in 1959 and hiring an agency full time for the 1979 election campaign. Since then all parties have developed more sophisticated campaigns, with badges often forming an integral part.

Margaret Thatcher, leader of the Conservative Party from 1975 and, from 1979, the first European woman prime minister, was viewed by her party as a distinct electoral asset. Her name appears on this official party badge (2). The text can be interpreted as the caring final words of a personal letter or as a simple injunction and the cross as a kiss or a vote. The message is clear: Thatcher is to be loved and elected. Another badge in the Conservative Party's traditional blue was distributed to constituency party helpers by

Jeffrey Archer, the party's deputy chairman in 1985-6 (3). When Archer had to resign, many examples remained in Conservative Central Office: 'We can't think of any conceivable use for them', a spokesperson was reported as saying.

4

The refining of the Labour Party's image in the mid 1980s caused the stylized red rose (4), long used by European socialist parties, to be replaced by the more naturalistic image seen on a badge issued by the National Union of Public Employees (NUPE), a trade union that would later amalgamate to become Unison (5). The change in Labour's image helped secure victory in the 1997 general election after eighteen years of Conservative governments. Another Labour win followed in 2001, when a central thrust of the Conservative Party's campaign was a call to retain the pound in the face of the euro (6), a policy that failed to engage the electorate.

5

1. *Send for Churchill, UK, 1951*
2. *Love Maggie, UK, about 1980*
3. *I'm a deputy, deputy chairman, UK, 1985/6*
4. *Labour women, UK, about 1985*
5. *NUPE for Labour, UK, 1987*
6. *Keep the pound, UK, 2001*

6

british politics

The proliferation of British badges in the 1960s was made possible by the emergence of a culture of protest and an accompanying trend towards more informal dress. Groups across the political spectrum have since used badges to promote their views.

Conservative government plans of the early 1970s to introduce museum entry charges were attacked in a campaign that here makes use of the Renaissance artist Leonardo da Vinci's self-portrait drawing (1). The 'social contract' agreed between the succeeding Labour government's Chancellor of the Exchequer Denis Healey and the trade unions is the target of a badge issued by the left-wing trade-unionist Rank and File Movement (2). In a 1981 contest for the deputy leadership of the Labour Party, Healey narrowly beat the left-wing Tony Benn, who was supported by the newspaper, *Socialist Challenge*, issuers of this badge (3). Although humorous, its intent was serious, for the party's future direction was felt to be at stake.

Increased unemployment under the Conservatives led to another humorous badge (4), its slogans taken from *Boys from the black stuff*, Alan Bleasdale's 1982 television dramas about unemployed Liverpudlians. The bicycle alludes to the Employment Secretary Norman Tebbit's suggestion that unemployed people should seek work on their bicycles. The idea that the same government might impose value added tax on books was countered by the National Book Committee (5). The community charge, or poll tax, introduced in 1989, was the target of many badges (6).

Campaigns of the 1980s concerning animal welfare used badges such as this, produced by the London-based group, Animus, in opposition to the hunting of foxes (7). In the late 1990s Labour government plans to outlaw fox-hunting came under attack from the Countryside Alliance, formed in 1998, which claimed that the government did not understand rural issues (8).

1

5

2

6

3

7

4

8

---

1. Campaign Against Museum Charges,
   UK, about 1972
2. No deal with Healey, UK, 1976
3. Tony Benn for deputy, UK, 1981
4. Gis a job, UK, about 1983

5. VAT on books is dangerous!, UK, 1984
6. Poll tax: you must be joking!, UK, 1988
7. Murder is a crime not a sport, UK,
   about 1985
8. Liberty and Livelihood, UK, 2002

american politics

1

2

The very different nature of the British and US political systems are reflected in badges. While the faces that have appeared on badges made for British elections generally belong to local parliamentary candidates, those on American badges have more often been national figures: the candidates for president and vice-president.

Early portraits issued during presidential election campaigns took the form of engravings or medals. In the 1848 elections photographs were used for the first time, and the development in 1856 of a process whereby a photographic image could be directly printed onto a sheet of iron enabled candidates to incorporate photographs of themselves into their campaign badges. Abraham Lincoln was among the first to make use of these new photographic badges. He was followed in 1868 by Ulysses S. Grant and his unsuccessful rival, the Democrat Horatio Seymour, who had himself and his vice-presidential nominee, Frank P. Blair, portrayed in this two-sided badge (1).

The arrival of the celluloid-covered button badge in the 1890s rapidly eclipsed this type of badge. Reporting on the presidential elections of 1896, the British *Strand Magazine* wrote that '"campaign buttons" adorn the lapels of voters all over the land'. The developer of the new process and leading badge manufacturer, Whitehead & Hoag, made this badge for the Republican president William H. Taft (2), who lost resoundingly in 1912.

Another manufacturing method, developed around 1914 and patented in 1917, was to print images directly onto the tin and protect them with a transparent coating. This FDR badge (3) was made by the Chicago-based Greenduck Company, using this process. The post Second World War badges illustrated here support Eisenhower, who won a second term of office in 1956 (4), and Kennedy and Nixon, rivals in the 1960 election (5, 6).

1. *H. Seymour and F.P. Blair, USA, 1868*
2. *William H. Taft, USA, probably 1912*
3. *Franklin Roosevelt, USA, probably 1936*
4. *Ike in '56, USA, 1956*
5. *Kennedy, USA, 1960*
6. *I'm for Dick Nixon, USA, 1960*

american politics

Since the nineteenth century political parties in the United States have used large, eye-catching badges to strengthen support and celebrate success.

This example (1), produced at the time of the re-election for a second term of office of the Republican president Ronald Reagan and vice-president George Bush, suggests that their first administration has seen the United States return to its former glory. No information is given on this earlier period, but a contrast is implied with the preceding presidency of Democrat Jimmy Carter and memories are evoked of the United States' inability to prevent the 1979 Russian invasion of Afghanistan and of the following year's failed rescue of fifty-three American hostages held in Tehran by Islamic militants. The badge's claim is that the optimism espoused by Reagan in his 1980 campaign has born fruit and the country's self-esteem has been restored.

A badge of eight years later (2) is remarkably similar in its message and its iconography, even though it is in support of the opposing party. The Democrat Bill Clinton and his vice-president Al Gore were elected after twelve years of Republican government and the badge promises yet another beginning. The imagery of smiling faces set against the American flag – and even the stars adorning the inscription – is the same. Regardless of policy differences, the two badges project an identical vision: a break with the immediate past, a feeling of wellbeing, and unassailable patriotism.

1. *Bringing America back, USA, 1984*
2. *A new voice for a new America,*
   USA, 1992

1

2

negative campaigns

As well as using badges to enhance their own public image, political parties have not hesitated to employ them to pour scorn on their opponents. The British Labour Party used a caricature of Margaret Thatcher by Ralph Steadman (1), while this Conservative Party badge (2) helped secure a third successive win against Labour in 1987.

Negative campaigning has also been a constant feature of American politics, with the use of disrespectful badges growing in the last quarter of the twentieth century as a consequence of the rise of the various protest movements. The Watergate scandal, which arose after Republican agents were arrested following an attempt to tap telephone lines in Democratic Party headquarters, led to many badges demanding the resignation and impeachment of President Richard Nixon. This example (3) refers to the swearing in the White House recordings of Nixon's conversations about the affair. Having been forced to hand over the tapes that revealed he had lied, and with the impeachment process gathering force, Nixon resigned in August 1974.

Two subsequent presidents are ridiculed in badges that compare Jimmy Carter's performance as president with the antics of the 1930s comic team, the Marx brothers (4), and Ronald Reagan with Bonzo, the chimpanzee in Reagan's 1951 film, *Bedtime for Bonzo* (5). The road traffic sign is an immediately comprehensible shorthand commonly used by badge designers. A later badge (6) relates to an investigation into the activities of President Clinton, his wife Hillary and their associates regarding the Whitewater Development Corporation. The slogan refers back to Nixon's famous promise in his televised address of 1973, that in the Watergate investigations, 'There can be no whitewash at the White House'.

4

5

---

1. *Spoilsport, UK, about 1985*
2. *Labour's answer to a better Britain – no, UK, 1987*
3. *Impeach Richard Nixon, USA, 1974*
4. *Carter is doing the job of three men, USA, about 1978*
5. *No Bonzos, USA, 1984*
6. *Don't whitewash Whitewater, USA, about 1993*

6

national politics

POVO-MFA

Party badges have long been used around the world as a means of consolidating support. The Swedish Social Democratic Party has issued a May Day badge annually since the 1890s. This example shows the statesman Hjalmar Branting (1). In the 1930s the German Nazi Party also issued badges. This particular example (2) was sold as a party fund-raiser on the Munich streets on Sunday 18 July 1937, the *Tag der deutschen Kunst* (Day of German Art).

This badge of the Portuguese Armed Forces Movement (Movimento das Forças Armadas or MFA) was issued around the time of the 1975 Portuguese elections (3). The MFA, formed by discontented junior army officers in 1973 and prominent in the 1974 revolution, was a leading political force. The badge stresses the shared interests of the army and the people (*povo*). Khalq (4) was one of the communist groups that deposed the king of Afghanistan in the 1978 revolution and was foremost in the country's government until the Soviet invasion of 1979. Both the socialist PASOK (5) and the conservative New Democracy (6) parties were founded in 1974, following the collapse of military rule in Greece.

These two South African badges, showing Frederik Willem de Klerk (7) and Nelson Mandela (8), were issued for the country's first multiracial elections, held in 1994. De Klerk, who, as president, had overseen Mandela's release from prison in 1990, was superseded by Mandela after the African National Congress won a sweeping victory. The Hindu nationalist Bharatiya Janata (Indian People's) Party (9) formed a coalition government after performing strongly in India's 1998 elections – the world's largest.

1. *Social Democratic Party, Sweden, 1935*
2. *National Socialist Party, Germany, 1937*
3. *Armed Forces Movement, Portugal, about 1975*
4. *Khalq Party, Afghanistan, 1978/9*
5. *Pan-Hellenic Socialist Movement, Greece, about 1989*
6. *New Democracy Party, Greece, about 1989*
7. *National Party, South Africa, 1994*
8. *African National Congress, South Africa, 1994*
9. *Bharatiya Janata Party, India, 1998*

7

8

9

chinese politics

Political badges have an important role to play in countries that do not hold elections. Badges of Mao Zedong had been made in China since the 1940s, but from the beginning of the Cultural Revolution in 1966 their numbers mushroomed as the cult of Chairman Mao was officially encouraged. Production was not monopolized by the government, and all sorts of bodies, from businesses and factories to army units and schools, were allowed to initiate their own designs. It has been estimated that at this time over ninety per cent of the population had a Mao badge pinned to the chest, and their variety ensured that badge collecting became a popular pursuit.

The badges served to confirm the authority of the figure who, as leader of the Chinese Communist Party (CCP), had been instrumental in founding the People's Republic of China in 1949. Some portrayed him as a quasi-divine figure, with rays emanating from his head. This example (1) commemorates forty-eight years of the CCP. Behind the waving figure of Mao are three potent symbolic places: the mountains of Jinggangshan (the first revolutionary base, established in 1927), the pagoda at Yan'an (where the Long March of 1934-5 ended), and Tian'anmen, from where Mao announced the foundation of the People's Republic. On the back is 'Long live Chairman Mao' in English and Chinese.

By the time this badge was made, the situation had become out of hand. Badge production was taking priority over more vital needs and the country's stock of aluminium was running out. Government policy changed, and official disapproval meant that very few Mao badges were made after 1970, apart from a brief revival after Mao's death in 1976. An order was sent out that badges should be handed in to be recycled, but the many collections that exist in China today indicate that this instruction was not heeded by all.

1. *Mao Zedong, China, 1969*

russian politics

Cheaply produced badges in support of communism were manufactured in the Soviet Union (USSR) in large numbers from the 1960s. Lenin, who had led the October 1917 uprising, which brought the communists to power, and had been instrumental in creating the USSR in 1922, was a popular subject (1). In particular, 1970, the centenary of his birth, saw the production of many varieties.

This state of affairs was to change radically following the election of Mikhail Gorbachev to the post of general secretary of the Communist Party in 1985. The following year Gorbachev announced the introduction of *perestroika* (restructuring) and *glasnost* (openness), ushering in reforms that encouraged private ownership of businesses and agriculture, a decrease in government bureaucracy, and open elections. These reforms were intended to operate within the framework of the communist system, as is made clear by the presence of communist symbols, the star and hammer and sickle, on this badge celebrating *perestroika* (2). But events rapidly moved beyond this, as republics ceded from the Soviet Union throughout 1990 and 1991. Gorbachev, who served as president of the Soviet Union at this time (3), was powerless to prevent the break-up of the country.

In June 1990 Russia declared its sovereignty within the Soviet Union, and in the following June Boris Yeltsin was chosen as Russia's president in a democratic election. This badge (4), which predates the election (it was presented to the British Museum in May 1991), urges his suitability for the role. In spite of Yeltsin's anti-communist stance and his resignation from the Communist Party in July 1990, the badge retains the symbols of communism.

At the end of 1991 Gorbachev resigned and the Soviet Union was officially dissolved.

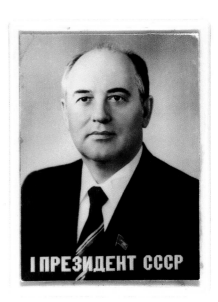

3

I ПРЕЗИДЕНТ СССР

4

1. *Lenin, USSR, about 1975*
2. *Perestroika, USSR, about 1988*
3. *USSR president Gorbachev, USSR, 1990/91*
4. *Russian president Yeltsin, USSR, 1990/91*

eastern european politics

The fall of communism in eastern Europe and its replacement by democratic elections on a western European model are reflected in badges of the 1980s and 1990s.

In 1981 martial law was declared in Poland as a response to the dramatic rise of Solidarity (Solidarnosc), an independent trade union formed the previous year. In the absence of protest badges, electrical resisters were used to signify opposition to this measure (1). These were generally worn covertly, as these symbols of resistance could result in the wearer's arrest. During the 1980s Solidarity badges proliferated, and the union's logo, as seen on this badge of the Mazowsze region (2), gained worldwide fame; the letters NSZZ on the badge stand for Independent Self-Governing Trade Union. Other popular subjects for Polish badges of the 1980s were Solidarity's founder and leader Lech Walesa (3) and the Roman Catholic priest and Solidarity supporter, Jerzy Popieluszko, murdered by agents of the state in October 1984 (4). In

1989 Solidarity was legalized, and in 1990 the communist general Wojciech Jaruzelski resigned as president of Poland. Lech Walesa was elected in his place, beating off rivals who included former prime minister Tadeusz Mazowiecki (5).

6

In 1978 the Czech Soviet Socialist Republic (CSSR) celebrated its thirtieth anniversary (6). Eleven years later, in the 1989 'velvet revolution' the Czech Communist Party was abolished and a government of national understanding was appointed. The opposition movment, Civic Forum (Obcanske Forum), played an important role in events and became the ruling party after the elections of 1990 (7). Both these elections and those of 1992 saw a plethora of competing parties (8).

7

8

1. *Resistance, Poland, 1981*
2. *Solidarity, Poland, about 1985*
3. *Lech Walesa, Poland, about 1985*
4. *Anniversary of the death of Jerzy Popieluszko, Poland, 1985*
5. *Tadeusz Mazowiecki, Poland, 1990*
6. *30th anniversary of the CSSR, Czechoslovakia, 1978*
7. *Civic Forum, Czechoslovakia, 1990*
8. *Czechoslovak Socialist Party, Czechoslovakia, 1992*

british trade unions

Badges have played various roles in the history of British trade unionism. The system of issuing quarterly badges to paid-up members was taken up by the Lancashire and Cheshire Miners' Federation during its membership drive of 1910-14 (1). Provided with holes, the badges could be stitched to clothing.

Other badges celebrate the trade union movement and raise funds. For the centenary of the Tolpuddle martyrs – six agricultural labourers transported to Australia in 1834 for forming a trade union – the Trades Union Congress (TUC) initiated a competition for a commemorative medal, which was judged by a panel that included the sculptor Eric Gill and won by a Birmingham badge designer, E.J. Fey. The design was used for a centenary banner and for badges (2).

The original TUC of 1868 consisted of craft-based unions, but the affiliation in the 1880s and 1890s of newer unions of unskilled workers resulted in more socialist policies. The Amalgamated Society of Engineers, Machinists, Smiths, Millwrights and Patternmakers was one of the older unions, founded in 1851. Its relative conservatism is reflected in the motto, 'Defence not Defiance' (3). In contrast this two-sided badge of the National Union of Railwaymen employs the final words of Karl Marx's 1848 *Communist Manifesto*: 'Workers of the world unite' (4). The figure on the Electrical Trades Union badge (5) is based on the 'angel of freedom' designed in 1898 for the union's banner by the painter and illustrator Walter Crane. The lace-up boot, court shoe and pair of stilettos on the three badges of the National Union of Boot and Shoe Operatives (6-8) illustrate changing fashions in women's shoes.

1. *Lancashire and Cheshire Miners' Federation, UK, 1910/14*
2. *Tolpuddle martyrs centenary, UK, 1934*
3. *Amalgamated Society of Engineers, UK, about 1913*
4. *National Union of Railwaymen, UK, about 1920s*
5. *Electrical Trades Union, UK, early 20th century*
6-8. *National Union of Boot and Shoe Operatives, UK, about 1900, 1935, 1960*

british trade unions

1

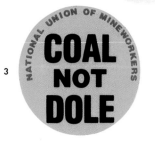

2

3

Badges have played a key role in many union campaigns. Throughout the 1980s British unions opposed many of the policies of the Conservative government of Margaret Thatcher, including the introduction of legislation curbing union power and the privatization of public utilities. But the unions' strength was diminished by the decline in membership that these policies brought about. The increase in the number of unemployed people in the early years of the decade was highlighted by the Trades Union Congress (TUC) in its 'Give us a future' campaign against youth unemployment (1) and the 'People's march for jobs' of 1983, in which five hundred unemployed men and women marched from Glasgow to London (2). The representation of a minuscule Thatcher fleeing before the mighty TUC 'Jobs Express' was hardly an accurate indication of the relative strengths of the unions and government. The road logo on the 1983 badge also appeared on T-shirts, banners and commemorative mugs.

High-profile labour disputes of the 1980s included the long-lasting and acrimonious – and ultimately unsuccessful – miners' strike of 1984-85 in opposition to proposed pit closures, which resulted in hundreds of badges (3). The campaign to reinstate trade unions in the intelligence-gathering Government Communications Headquarters in Cheltenham, banned by the government in 1984, also saw the production of many badges, including this one issued by the Council of Civil Service Unions (4). Other campaigns were organized against the closure of British Rail's Swindon works, announced in 1985 (5), against the privatisation of the water industry, which took place in 1989 (6), and against the removal of News International's newspaper production to Wapping in east London and the dismissal of staff (7). The barbed wire on this badge alludes to the defences erected around the site.

4

5

6

---

1. *Youth against Thatcher, UK, about 1982*
2. *People's march for jobs, UK, 1983*
3. *Coal not dole, UK, 1984*
4. *GCHQ trade unions, UK, 1984/5*
5. *Defend the rail works, UK, about 1985*
6. *Water works, UK, 1986*
7. *Official Wapping Picket, UK, 1986/7*

7

american trade unions

In the early years of the twentieth century American trade unions issued elaborate badges in which many different materials and production techniques were combined. These badges were made possible by the development of the button badge and used cheap materials in an attempt to ape the grandeur of the traditional badge of office (right). This example (1) was supplied by the manufacturer Whitehead & Hoag in an envelope on which were listed no fewer than fifteen patents taken out between 1892 and 1897 to cover the company's badges. The envelope also proclaimed the diversity of the company's wares: 'Badges, banners, flags, buttons, advertising novelties'.

This badge was produced for use by one of the Cleveland, Ohio, branches (or locals) of an American dockworkers' union. Founded in 1892, this union was officially recognized the following year by the American Federation of Labor (AFL), the trade union umbrella group set up in 1886. In 1895, in order to include its Canadian members, the union's name was changed from the National Longshoremen's Association of the United States to the International Longshoremen's Association, the name by which the union is still known – although for a brief period, from 1901 to 1908, it took on the longer name given on this badge. The clasped hands that appear on the upper bar are a symbol of solidarity commonly found on trade union badges (and on earlier medals of friendly societies). The words 'Honest work shows a label' refers to the union label that appears on those American badges produced by unionized labour; on this badge the label is placed above the words 'Cleveland, Ohio'.

Presidential badge of the Anti-Gallican Society, UK, about 1750. Gold, silver, enamel and rock crystal are among the materials employed in this patriotic anti-French badge. Elaborate badges such as this inspired much cheaper twentieth-century versions.

1. *International Longshoremen, Marine and Transportworkers' Association, USA, about 1905*

american trade unions

As in Britain, US trade union badges have had various functions. This badge indicates that the wearer is a fully paid-up member of the Steel Workers Organizing Committee (1). This body was formed in 1936, a direct result of the foundation during the previous year of the Committee of Industrial Organization (CIO), set up to organize unskilled workers in the mass-production industries. The refusal of some employers to recognize the union resulted in strike action in May 1937, the month in which this membership badge was issued.

In 1955 the CIO merged with the older American Federation of Labor (AFL); this 1964 badge (2) indicates that the wearer has contributed to the organization's Committee on Political Education (COPE). The 1965 badge of the radical socialist union, Industrial Workers of the World (IWW) (3), commemorates the fiftieth anniversary of the execution of IWW member and political songwriter Joe Hill, executed in 1915. The words, 'Don't mourn

– organize' are taken from a telegram sent by Hill shortly before his death.

Three badges from the 1970s relate to specific campaigns. A motto pledging non-violence and a photograph of Cesar Chavez, leader of the United Farm Workers (UFW), appear on a badge backing the Californian grape-pickers' lengthy campaign for recognition of the UFW and improved working conditions (4). A badge bearing a caricature of the owner of the *Washington Post*, Katherine Graham, weighing pressmen against profits was made at the time of a bitter strike by that newspaper's workers (5). Another, issued as part of the Amalgamated Clothing and Textile Workers Union's long campaign against textile manufacturer J.P. Stevens, shows a worker who had died of brown lung disease the previous year (6).

4

5

---

1. *Steel Workers Organizing Committee, USA, 1937*
2. *I gave to COPE, USA, 1964*
3. *Don't mourn – organize, USA, 1965*
4. *Non-violence is our strength, USA, about 1973*
5. *Defend the pressmen!, USA, 1975/6*
6. *Help textile workers win justice, USA, 1979*

6

war

A surge of popular imperialist feeling in Britain around 1900 resulted in the production of patriotic badges celebrating the war between Britain and the two Boer republics formed in southern Africa by Dutch colonists in the mid nineteenth century. The conflict began in 1899 and ended with victory for Britain in 1902. The Boer republics were incorporated into the British Empire and would later become South Africa.

An ornate badge was produced to advertise a bazaar held in London's Kensington to support the British war effort (1). Described on the badge as a tribute from the British Empire to Queen Victoria (who is pictured) and her armed forces, the 'defenders' of British interests, the bazaar was opened by Princess Alexandra on 24 May 1900. A printed paper disc inserted into the back reads: 'Pray do your duty and sell your friends a Badge'. Another badge juxtaposes the British flag and the arms of the City of London to celebrate the return from the war of the City of London Imperial Volunteers (CIVs) in October 1900 (2). The soldiers' homecoming was marked by such jubilation that their triumphal march through London descended into chaos, as crowds spilled into their path.

Many badges praise Lord Roberts, commander-in-chief of the British forces from January 1900: this example marks the British occupation of the Boer capital, Pretoria, in June that year (3). Others contain more general patriotic messages quoting from Nelson's exhortation at the Battle of Trafalgar of 1805 (4), Sir Lewis Morris's *Song of Empire*, composed for Queen Victoria's 1887 golden jubilee (5), and George Essex Evans' imperialist poem of 1899, *The lion's whelps* (6). Ironically, these badges were made in the United States: that of Lord Roberts by Baldwin & Gleason of New York and the three smaller badges by Whitehead & Hoag.

3

4

5

6

1. *National Bazaar, probably USA, 1900*
2. *Welcome home, gallant CIVs, USA or UK, 1900*
3. *General Roberts, USA, 1900*
4. *England expects, USA, about 1900*
5. *We hold a vaster empire, USA, about 1900*
6. *Let the hunters 'ware, USA, about 1900*

war

The First and Second World Wars both saw the production of patriotic badges in Britain and America. By the First World War button badges had been made in Britain for over a decade. This example, manufactured by the Merchants' Portrait Company of north London, commemorates Lord Kitchener (1), who had succeeded Lord Roberts as commander-in-chief of the British forces in the Boer War in November 1900, and was appointed Secretary of State for War at the outbreak of the First World War. A popular figure, he appeared on the famous 'Your country needs you' army recruitment poster. He died in June 1916, when the ship he was travelling on was sunk by a German mine. Other British badges of the time featured the leaders of allied countries (2), while in the United States badges were used to mobilize support for the Liberty Loan campaigns, which raised money for the war effort (3).

Many American badges of the Second World War refer back to the Japanese bombing of the US naval base at Pearl Harbor, Hawaii, in December 1941, the event that brought the United States into the war (4). The memory of this surprise attack helped ensure continuing popular support for American involvement in the war.

Badges have also been produced in support of more recent conflicts and the soldiers fighting them. This American example was issued by the organization, Veterans of Foreign Wars (VFW), as part of its response to protests against the Vietnam War (5). A British badge was issued by the Friends of the Falklands Committee after the Falkland Islands, invaded by Argentinian forces in April 1982, had been recaptured by Britain two months later (6).

4

5

6

1. *Deeds not words, UK, 1916*
2. *Albert I, king of Belgium, UK, about 1916*
3. *Get behind the government, USA, 1917*
4. *Remember Pearl Harbor, USA, about 1942*
5. *USA – love it or leave it, USA, about 1966*
6. *Britannia rules OK, UK, 1982*

peace

Badges praising peace have a shorter history than those supporting war, becoming common only since the 1960s and the rise of the modern peace movement, a development that was fuelled by widespread anxieties over the risks posed by nuclear weapons. The foremost British organization working in this field has been the Campaign for Nuclear Disarmament (CND), founded in 1958. Its activities during the 1960s included sit-ins and blockades, organized by its direct action group, the Committee of 100 (1), and annual marches between Aldermaston, home of the Atomic Weapons Research Establishment, and London (2, 3). The CND emblem was designed by Gerald Holtom and combines the semaphore signals for the letters N and D; it has since gained popularity worldwide.

CND's membership grew rapidly in the early 1980s, following the Conservative government's decision to deploy US Cruise missiles and commission Trident nuclear submarines. A Conservative Party badge (4) counters CND's call for unilateral nuclear disarmament, replacing the popular slogan, 'Nuclear power no thanks', with a demand for Russian disarmament. Ironically, the same message appears on a CND badge of the same year bearing the Russian word 'No' (5), one of a series naming various American and Russian nuclear weapons (6). Other CND badges of the 1980s publicize demonstrations in Barrow-in-Furness, where Trident submarines were to be constructed (7), and London (8); this badge features a mutated sheep by cartoonist Steve Bell.

A later badge issued by the Committee for Peace in the Balkans (9) protests against the NATO bombing of Yugoslavia, which followed attacks by Serbian-dominated Yugoslav forces on Kosovar Albanians. The target symbol, used in Belgrade by protestors against the bombing, was taken up by opponents to the military action in other countries.

1. Committee of 100, UK, about 1960
2. Youth CND Aldermaston march, UK, 1965
3. Aldermaston march, UK, 1968
4. Soviet missiles no thanks, UK, 1983
5. No to SS20, UK, 1983
6. Refuse Cruise, UK, 1983
7. Stop Trident, UK, 1984
8. March for a nuclear free Britain, UK, 1987
9. Peace in the Balkans, UK, 1999

peace

Images of the destruction wrought by the atomic bombs dropped on the Japanese cities of Hiroshima and Nagasaki in 1945 and the continuing proliferation of yet more powerful nuclear arms in the years following the Second World War led to demands for the abolition of such weapons. This was a key goal of the peace movements that developed in Europe, north America and Australasia from the 1960s.

A bilingual Canadian badge (1) commemorating Hiroshima Day (6 August), the anniversary of the first use of a nuclear bomb, was produced for the international exhibition, Expo '67, held in Montreal. The image is of a joyous crowd celebrating peace. By contrast, two badges produced in the United States some fifteen years later employ dark humour: on one the words that customarily closed Warner Brothers' cartoons appear over the mushroom cloud of an atomic explosion (2), whilst the other maintains the impossibility of surviving a nuclear war (3).

No image deflects the attention from the urgent message on a Dutch badge of 1986 (4): 'Don't be a party to Woensdrecht! Cruise missiles never! Demonstrate on Saturday 17 May!' In 1979 the Dutch government had agreed to the installation of US nuclear Cruise missiles at a military base near the town of Woensdrecht if no arms control agreement had been reached by November 1985; construction work duly began at the base on 26 April 1986. The badge also voices opposition to 'Star Wars', the US Strategic Defense Initiative announced in 1983, which many felt would increase the likelihood of nuclear war rather than offer protection against it.

3

4

1. *Hiroshima Day, Canada, 1967*
2. *That's all folks!, USA, 1982*
3. *See one nuclear war you've seen them all, USA, 1983*
4. *Don't be a party to Woensdrecht!, Netherlands, 1986*

war in vietnam

During the 1960s peace campaigners in the United States focussed their attentions particularly on the war in Vietnam. The first US troops arrived in Vietnam in 1961, and the war against the communist North Vietnamese was executed vigorously from 1964 until a cease-fire was negotiated in 1973 and the US withdrawal began. An estimated two million lives were lost in the conflict.

The American decision to pull out of the war resulted from a failure to inflict lasting damage on the North Vietnamese forces, and also from opposition to the war within the United States. This opposition grew as the cost of the war increased in terms of both American soldiers' lives and the suffering of the Vietnamese people. The plight of Vietnamese civilians in the face of American air power is vividly portrayed in this badge (1), whilst the mounting death toll of American soldiers is suggested by the US flag flying at half-mast alongside a simple inscription that leaves open the closing date of the war (2). The swing in public opinion that hastened the American withdrawal showed itself in massive demonstrations organized by the various mobilization committees. Badges played a part in publicizing these events. This example (3) was designed by the celebrated sculptor Alexander Calder for the New Mobilization Committee, for what was at the time the largest anti-war march ever, held in Washington D.C.; at the same time other demonstrations were held in cities throughout America. Other artists produced works opposing the war. A drawing by David Levine condemning the continuing bombing of Vietnam, which appeared first in the *New York Review of Books*, was later used on a badge issued by the National Peace Action Coalition (4): US president Richard Nixon is shown riding on a bomber and waving a bomb that parodies the well-known symbol of nuclear disarmament.

3

4

---

1. *Out now, USA, 1969*
2. *Vietnam 1961-, USA, 1969*
3. *New Mobilization, USA, 1969*
4. *President Nixon as a bomber, USA, 1971*

war in the gulf

The 1990 Iraqi invasion of Kuwait and its subsequent defeat by a multinational force led by the United States provoked much debate worldwide. Directly opposing views are expressed in two badges issued by the London-based Free Kuwait Campaign (1) and Hands Off Iraq Committee (2). Whereas the latter body wholeheartedly supported the Iraqi leader Saddam Hussein, most British organizations opposing the war urged a peaceful solution to the crisis or criticized western motives. The view that the international response resulted from an interest in Kuwait's huge oil reserves is voiced in a badge issued by the Socialist Workers' Party (3). In striking contrast to this is an American badge celebrating the military campaign Desert Storm (4), whilst a British badge wrongly predicts that Saddam Hussein's rule will soon end (5).

The allied attack on Iraq of 2003 was preceded by no Iraqi act of aggression equivalent to its earlier invasion of Kuwait, and European public opposition to the war was strengthened by a widespread belief that Iraq did not pose a threat to international security. In Britain the firm of Better Badges supplied the Stop The War Coalition with two hundred thousand badges of various designs, including this (6); the individual who donated this example to the British Museum had worn it on a London march of 15 February 2003, in which around a million people took part. The image of the missile cancelled by a diagonal line was used internationally as a symbol of opposition to the war. It recurs on a badge issued by the Catalan Fundació per la Pau (Peace Foundation) (7). This example was acquired in Barcelona, a city in which opposition to the war was particularly strong, with banners bearing this image hanging from many balconies.

1. *Free Kuwait, UK, 1990*
2. *Hands off Iraq!, UK, 1990*
3. *No blood for oil, UK, 1991*
4. *Desert Storm, USA, 1991*
5. *Saddam your time is up, UK, 1991*
6. *Don't attack Iraq, UK, 2003*
7. *Let's stop the war, Spain, 2003*

south africa

South Africa's apartheid system of government was the target of international protest from the 1960s to the 1980s. The country's racist laws, which aimed to maintain the domination of the country's white population, were first instituted in 1948 and were extended in the 1960s. As a result, groups around the world campaigned for the political and economic isolation of the country while apartheid remained in place.

These groups included student organizations, for example, the Southern Africa Solidarity Committee, formed at Harvard University in the United States in 1977, which called for the university to dispose of its South African investments (1). British protests were headed by the Anti-Apartheid Movement (AAM), which was founded in 1959 and organized on many fronts. A key demand was for the release from prison of African National Congress (ANC) leaders such as Nelson Mandela (2). The ANC, the main focus of opposition to the system within South Africa, had been outlawed in 1960, and Mandela was sentenced to life imprisonment in 1964. The AAM also organized such events as a demonstration in June 1984 against the visit to London of the South African prime minister Pieter Willem Botha; featured on the badge announcing this march is the organization's symbolic black and white AA emblem (3). Trade unions also campaigned on this issue, as illustrated by this British badge, which also makes effective use of black and white (4). An American badge, issued soon after Mandela's release from prison by the Capital District Coalition Against Apartheid and Racism, a group based in Albany, New York State, demands the application of economic sanctions until the apartheid system is finally renounced (5).

3

4

5

1. *No Harvard dollars for apartheid, USA, 1978*
2. *Free Nelson Mandela, UK, about 1984*
3. *No to Botha!, UK, 1984*
4. *Stop oil supplies to South Africa, UK, about 1986*
5. *Sanctions now!, USA, 1990*

the global village

Just as the Anti-Apartheid Movement was formed to campaign against apartheid in South Africa, other groups of varying sizes and strengths were formed in Britain in the 1960s and 1970s to fight perceived injustices in other countries around the world.

This badge (1) was issued as part of a campaign to free what was then Rhodesia from white minority rule. The former British colony had declared independence unilaterally in 1965; the denial of voting rights to the black population is expressed on the badge by a white gag. Following international and internal pressure, the first multi-racial elections were held in 1980, a black government was installed, and the country's name was changed to Zimbabwe. The Chile Solidarity Campaign (2) was established in Britain in 1974, following the September 1973 coup that replaced the elected left-wing government of President Salvador Allende with a military junta headed by General Augusto Pinochet. The Campaign Against Repression in Iran (CARI) was launched in

1975 in opposition to the repressive policies of the shah of Iran; this badge (3) opposes the sale of British *Chieftain* tanks to the shah, who was deposed in 1979 before the sale could go ahead. The Nicaragua Solidarity Campaign was formed in 1978, and supported Nicaragua's left-wing Sandinista movement, which wrested power from the Somoza dictatorship the following year. Throughout the 1980s the organization campaigned against US support for the Nicaraguan contras, rebels opposed to the Sandinistas. The badge shows the early twentieth-century Nicaraguan revolutionary Augusto Cesar Sandino, after whom the movement took its name (4). Amnesty International (5) was founded in Britian during 1961 as a politically impartial organization campaigning on behalf of political prisoners around the world.

1. Liberate Zimbabwe, UK, about 1974
2. Solidarity with the people of Chile, UK,
   about 1975
3. No arms for the shah, UK, about 1978
4. No US intervention Nicaragua, UK,
   about 1986
5. Amnesty International, UK, about 1985

the global village

As in Britain, pressure groups in the United States have used badges to address international issues since the 1960s. Some campaigns, such as that opposing the war in Vietnam, have demanded change from the US government, whilst some have been directed towards the rulers of foreign countries, which in the 1970s and '80s included the racist government of South Africa and the military regime in Chile. Concerns relating to other parts of the world are illustrated here.

This badge (1) was issued by the American Committee to Keep Biafra Active at the time of the three-year war that followed Biafra's declaration of independence from Nigeria in 1967; the Biafrans experienced severe famine and eventual defeat. The Irish Northern Aid Committee, or Noraid, was formed in 1970 to raise funds for Irish republican prisoners and their families; this badge demands that British Northern Ireland, depicted in orange, be reunited with the

1

2

rest of Ireland (2). The badge of the Venceremos Brigade, an organization founded in 1969 to foster links with socialist Cuba, proclaims two of its key demands: the evacuation by US forces of the Guantanamo Bay naval base, first leased from the Cuban government in 1903, and an end to the US economic blockade of Cuba (3). A badge from the New York office of Mobilization for Survival, a network of groups campaigning on peace and justice issues, opposes US support for the right-wing government of Salvador, established in 1979 after a military coup (4). The Student Struggle for Soviet Jewry was formed in New York in 1964 to campaign for the rights of Jews living in Russia and the rest of the Soviet Union; their situation is symbolized here by a star of David appearing imprisoned within a communist star (5).

1. *Recognize Biafra, USA, 1969*
2. *Unite Ireland, USA, 1972*
3. *End the blockade of Cuba, USA, 1973*
4. *Hands off El Salvador, USA, 1981*
5. *Free Soviet Jews, USA, about 1981*

neighbourhood
and nation

Badges have been widely used on a local, as well as an international, level. People's Park was created as a community park in 1969 in Berkeley, California. A campaign to preserve it from development led to violent clashes with police and gained worldwide attention (1). Another badge focusses on Proposition P, which would have restricted high-rise developments in San Francisco (2): King Kong is shown on the city's Transamerica Pyramid, completed in 1972, rather than in New York, as in the 1933 film *King Kong*. This British badge (3) was issued by admirers of Brighton's nineteenth-century West Pier, closed in 1975 and at risk of demolition. Another (4), showing a London bus against the London Transport symbol, was part of a short-lived campaign urging the non-payment of fares, after the Labour-led Greater London Council (GLC) was forced to reverse its 1981 'Fares Fair' policy of lower fares on public transport. Following the Conservative government's 1983 announcement of its plan to abolish the

GLC, the council campaigned vigorously to save itself (5).

British badges have also been concerned with broader issues of sovereignty. A badge of the Troops Out Movement, formed in the early 1970s to work for the removal of British troops from Northern Ireland, shows Britain as an armed soldier striking Ireland (6). In contrast, a Federation of Conservative Students badge uses a union flag in the shape of Northern Ireland to suggest its affinity with Britain (7). Concerns that the European Union might in turn encroach on British sovereignty are voiced in a badge issued by *This England* magazine (8). The organization Scottish Watch also uses a national flag, but here it is the saltire, symbolizing Scottish identity in the face of 'English exploitation' (9).

5

6

7

8

---

1. *Defend the park!, USA, about 1969*
2. *Vote yes on P, USA, 1972*
3. *We want the West Pier, UK, about 1980*
4. *Don't pay the fare increases, UK, 1982*
5. *Keep GLC, UK, about 1983*
6. *Troops out now!, UK, about 1983*
7. *Loyal Ulster, UK, about 1985*
8. *Don't let Europe rule Britannia, UK, 1990*
9. *Scottish Watch, UK, 1993*

9

the environment

Concerns over the future of the earth have led to campaigns and badges on a wide range of environmental issues since the 1970s.

Most of the 1980s badges shown here express anxieties over nuclear power. This American badge (1) publicizes a six-day protest walk across New Jersey, which took place on the second anniversary of a near-meltdown at the Three Mile Island nuclear power plant near Harrisburg, Pennsylvania. The dollar sign suggests that the plant's owners, General Public Utilities, prioritized profits over safety. The Three Mile Island incident and the suspicion that the truth surrounding it had not been made public increased anti-nuclear feeling worldwide. On a badge designed by cartoonist Jules Feiffer and issued by Harrisburg's Labor Committee for Safe Energy and Full Employment (2), the succinct message and radioactive cloud above a cooling tower suggest official deceit around the subject. A British badge (3) copying an American design implies that a similar disaster could occur anywhere.

The smiling sun device was first used in Aarhus, Denmark, in 1975. The anti-nuclear group, Organisationen til Oplysning om Atomkraft, issued smiling sun badges with the words 'Nuclear power? No thanks' in over forty languages (4). The rainbow colours of this Danish Greenpeace badge became another popular symbol (5); the international organization Greenpeace was founded in 1971 to campaign on environmental issues.

The 1986 explosion at the Chernobyl nuclear power plant in Ukraine, then part of the Soviet Union, devastated large areas of land, and many thousands had to be evacuated from contaminated areas. This mnemonic badge, issued in Britain by the Campaign for Nuclear Disarmament, points to the long-lasting effects of the disaster (6). Another British badge, issued by the Anti Nuclear Campaign, opposes the construction of Britain's first pressurized water nuclear reactor (PWR) at Sizewell in Suffolk, begun in 1987 after a public enquiry lasting more than two years (7).

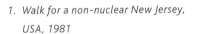

1. Walk for a non-nuclear New Jersey, USA, 1981
2. They lie, USA, 1981
3. We all live in Pennsylvania, UK, about 1981
4. Nuclear power? No thanks, Denmark, about 1984
5. Stop acid rain, Denmark, about 1984
6. Chernobyl never disappears, UK, about 1987
7. PWR – stop now!, UK, about 1988

race

Art work for a badge of the Black Panther, Bobby Hutton, USA, 1968. In the photograph Hutton and a comrade are both wearing badges

Badges reflect the differing ways in which groups have sought to tackle racist oppression and bigotry.

The Black Panther Party, formed in California in 1966, adopted violence as a means of achieving its goals. This badge shows Bobby Hutton, a Black Panther Party member shot by police in California in 1968 (1). It was made by Robert Rush, a Californian political activist and badge-maker, and is from a group given by Rush to the British Museum in 1997, along with associated art work (left). A member of the Black Panther and Communist Parties, the radical feminist Angela Davis was fired as a philosophy lecturer at the University of California in 1970 and arrested later the same year in connection with an attempted rescue of a group of black prisoners. An international campaign demanded Davis's release (2). After sixteen months in prison, she was acquitted in 1972.

Many British organizations, including local authorities, have issued anti-racist badges, but two organizations have been particularly active. Launched in 1976 following comments made by Eric Clapton in support of Enoch Powell's anti-immigration beliefs, Rock Against Racism aimed to promote racial harmony through music (3). It worked closely with the Anti Nazi League, formed in 1977 to oppose the right-wing National Front (NF), which was then increasing in strength (4). Similarly, a revival of the racist Ku Klux Klan was the occasion for the production of this American badge issued by the National Anti-Klan Network, a body founded in 1979 (5). The espousal of non-violence in Martin Luther King's celebrated 'I have a dream' speech is the subtext behind a badge issued by a local branch of the American Federation of State, County and Municipal Employees to mark a massive rally held in Washington DC on the twentieth anniversary of the speech (6).

1. *Bobby Hutton, USA, 1968*
2. *Free Angela Davis, UK, about 1971*
3. *Rock against Racism, UK, about 1978*
4. *Stop the NF nazis!, UK, about 1979*
5. *National Anti-Klan Network, USA, 1981*
6. *Martin Luther King, USA, 1983*

sexual politics

The first badges to address the status of women focussed on campaigns promoting the right of women to vote.

One of the principal British organizations was the Women's Social and Political Union (WSPU), formed by Emmeline Pankhurst and her daughters Christabel and Sylvia in 1903. The WSPU was prepared to use violent means in support of its aims, and as a result of such illegal activities as smashing windows and arson, 'suffragettes', as they came to be called from 1906, were locked up in London's Holloway Prison. On their release the women were presented by the WSPU with a silver and enamelled badge, the so-called 'Holloway brooch'. Designed by Sylvia Pankhurst in 1909, it features a portcullis pierced by a prison arrow in WSPU colours (1). From that year some of the imprisoned women went on hunger strikes, and as a result underwent feeding by force. Hunger-strikers received a silver medal hanging from a ribbon also in WSPU colours (2); the

1

inside lid of the box of this example reads: 'Presented to Joan Cather by the Women's Social & Political Union in recognition of a gallant action, whereby through endurance to the last extremity of hunger and hardship, a great principle of political justice was vindicated.' The badges issued by the WSPU took various forms. Whereas the hunger-strikers' medals appropriated the male language of military awards, the 'Holloway brooch' resembled a piece of jewellery, as did the miniature silver toffee-hammer brooches presented to those who had broken windows. Button badges bearing portraits of the Pankhursts were also issued.

Other groups to issue badges included the National Union of Women's Suffrage Societies and the Women's Tax Resistance League. In America the National Woman's Party's 'Jailed for Freedom' badge, with its prison gate secured by a chain, performed a similar role to the 'Holloway brooch'; its appearance owes an obvious debt to its British counterpart.

2

1. WSPU 'Holloway brooch', UK, about 1912
2. WSPU hunger strike award, UK, 1912

sexual politics

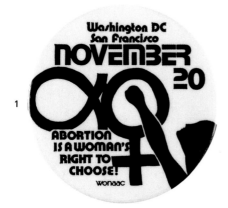

The proliferation of feminist activity in Britain and the United States from the late 1960s resulted in the production of a large number of badges from the 1970s on. Equal pay with men and the right to abortions on demand have been two key concerns.

This American badge issued by the Women's National Abortion Action Coalition (WONAAC) in 1971 to publicize a protest march combines the Greek letter alpha, for abortion, a female symbol, and the silhouette of a protestor (1), whilst a badge of the National Organization for Women, founded in 1966 to work for equality for women, shows the nineteenth-century women's rights campaigner Susan B. Anthony (2). By contrast, another US badge, issued by the group Black Women United for Political Action, consists solely of text (3).

The fist within a female symbol, adopted worldwide as a feminist symbol, appears in this British badge (4). Issued in support of a strike over equal pay by women workers at Trico, a London windscreen wiper manufacturer, the badge also proclaims the Working Women's Charter, which in 1974 had set out principles and priorities for achieving equality for women in the workplace. Another British badge (5) celebrates the last National Women's Liberation Conference, held in Birmingham in 1978; these conferences were held annually from 1970 until that year. The National Abortion Campaign (NAC) was set up in 1975 to counter attempts to restrict the 1967 Abortion Act, which had increased the availability of abortions in Britain; this NAC badge (6) opposes a bill introduced into Parliament by John Corrie in 1979.

More recent anti-abortion campaigners have responded with their own badges bearing such slogans as 'Protect unborn children' and 'Give life a chance'.

---

1. *A woman's right to choose!, USA, 1971*
2. *National Organization for Women, USA, 1972*
3. *Black Women United for Political Action, USA, 1977*
4. *Equal pay at Trico, UK, 1976*
5. *National Women's Liberation Conference, UK, 1978*
6. *Fight the Corrie bill!, UK, 1979*

sexual politics

The campaign for recognition and equality for gay men and lesbians came to prominence in the western world in the early 1970s.

The Gay Liberation Front (GLF) was formed in the United States in 1969, following the riots that followed police attempts to arrest employees of New York's gay Stonewall Inn. A GLF group was formed in Britain the following year. Its badge, with two male symbols and two female symbols interlinked over a clenched fist, is indicative of its militancy (1). Another device, the Greek letter lambda, which had been in use in New York from 1970, was adopted as an international symbol of lesbian and gay liberation in 1974 (2). A major British campaign of the 1970s was in support of *Gay News*, after Mary Whitehouse, founder of a 'Clean up TV campaign' and pictured on the badge, successfully sued the newspaper (3). The first US national march for lesbian and gay rights was held in Washington in 1979 (4).

A separate political identity for lesbians emerged during the second half of the 1970s (5), and in 1985 Britain's Gay Pride event, which had been held annually from 1970 (6), was renamed Lesbian and Gay Pride. In 1988 a group of lesbians abseiled into the House of Lords in protest against the introduction of a law stating that local authorities should not 'promote homosexuality'. The lesbians' action is alluded to in one of a series of badges issued by Trades Unionists Against Section 28, a group formed to fight the new law (7): here pink and black wedges, signifying the desired overturning of the measure, take the place of the more usual equilateral triangles, symbols of pride adopted from the badges that many gay men and lesbians were made to wear in Nazi Germany, the latter for 'anti-social behaviour'.

1. *Gay Liberation Front, UK, about 1973*
2. *Lambda, UK, about 1977*
3. *Gay News fights on!, UK, 1977*
4. *National march for lesbian and gay rights, USA, 1979*
5. *Lesbian Liberation, UK, about 1979*
6. *Gay Pride, UK, 1981*
7. *Abseil against Section 28, UK, 1989*

aids

The medical, social and political issues surrounding the worldwide AIDS epidemic have resulted in numerous badges. The condition was first documented in 1981, and in 1982 it was named Acquired Immune Deficiency Syndrome. Its cause was then unknown, but, as those first diagnozed with the disease in the United States and Britain were gay men, gay groups in those countries were prominent among the organizations providing education programmes and calling for increased resources for medical research. This badge (1) uses a symbolic road traffic warning sign and safety pins to encourage the practice of safer sex; it was issued by the London Lesbian & Gay Switchboard, a telephone advice service. An American badge (2) condemns prejudice directed against those with AIDS and at the same time stresses the need to find an effective vaccine and cure. A symbolic heart and arrow appear on this badge (3) issued by the Terrence Higgins Trust (THT); set up in

1982 and named after one of the first people to die of AIDS in Britain, THT was among the first British national bodies to campaign and advise on AIDS.

Red ribbons have been worn since 1991, when the Red Ribbon Project was set up by a New York group, Visual AIDS; the ribbons were intended to honour those who had died from AIDS, express solidarity with those living with the disease, educate the public, and raise funds for research and treatment. Their colour symbolizes blood, the medium by which the AIDS virus is passed, and also love. Since then, red ribbons have been used worldwide as symbols of AIDS awareness, as have badges based on them (4). In South Africa the traditional beadwork of the Ndebele people of southern Zimbabwe has been adapted to make badges bearing the symbol (5).

3

4

5

1. *Safer sex, UK, 1987*
2. *AIDS research not AIDS bigotry, USA, about 1990*
3. *Terrence Higgins Trust, UK, about 1994*
4. *AIDS awareness, UK, about 1993*
5. *AIDS awareness, South Africa, about 2002*

flag-days

Charities have long made use of badges, with flag-days a particularly effective means of raising funds.

During the First World War the badges given to contributors often took the form of small paper flags. The British and Foreign Sailors Society, which promoted the welfare of seamen and their dependents, held its flag-day on 21 October, the anniversary of Nelson's victory at the battle of Trafalgar in 1805; the flag shows the admiral's head against a cross of St George (1). The Star and Garter Home was established in 1916 in Richmond, Surrey, to care for severely disabled soldiers and sailors returning from the war (2).

Flowers have also been popular. Alexandra Rose Day was founded by Queen Alexandra in 1912. On its first flag-day, held in June that year, wild roses were sold in aid of various charities; since then it has been an annual event, with artificial roses replacing the more expensive blooms (3). The Royal British Legion, founded by Field

Marshal Douglas Haig in 1921 to help disabled ex-servicemen, held its first flag-day that November, selling artificial poppies, mementoes of those who had died in northern France in the First World War; many millions of these poppies are now made annually (4). In the 1930s the Co-operative Women's Guild responded by producing artificial white poppies, which were worn by pacifists who believed that remembrance was an inadequate response to war; the 1980s revival of the white poppy by the Peace Pledge Union provoked controversy in the press (5). The use of flowers on flag-days has now increased further, with real heather being sold in aid of children in Scotland (6) and artificial roses and daffodils in aid of arthritis and cancer charities respectively (7, 8).

5

6

7

8

---

1. *British and Foreign Sailors Society, UK, 1915*
2. *Star and Garter Home, UK, about 1916*
3. *Alexandra Rose Day, UK, 1985*
4. *Royal British Legion, UK, 1985*
5. *Peace Pledge Union, UK, 1988*
6. *Children 1st, UK, about 1995*
7. *Arthritis Research Campaign, UK, about 2003*
8. *Marie Curie Cancer Care, UK, about 2003*

status and office

Whilst political badges generally serve to announce one or more of the wearer's beliefs, a primary function of other badges is to identify his or her status. From the fourteenth century the senior members, or liverymen, of London's guilds were identified by their livery, which consisted of a special gown and sometimes a hood. But from the seventeenth century a general reluctance to wear these cumbersome uniforms, which had become old-fashioned and increasingly associated with the servant class, led to problems in identifying those entitled to attend the meetings called by London's lord mayor. Accordingly, many guilds instituted the practice of issuing their liverymen with medallic badges as an indication of their status. The Vintners' Company seems to have been the first to adopt this practice, beginning in 1769. A resolution to issue badges was passed by the Cutlers' Company in 1772, having been proposed by Thomas Dunnage, a past master of the guild; Dunnage's own badge is now in the British

Museum (1). The elephant relates to the use of ivory in cutlery. The use of badges to allow admittance has survived into modern times (2).

Other badges indicate different sorts of authority. This silver badge of office was formerly worn by staff in the British Museum's round Reading Room (3), whilst silver badges designed by Eric Gill identified Air Raid Precaution officers in the Second World War (4). More common has been the use of enamelled base metal, as in the badges presented by the Great Western Railway to new staff members (5) and those given by south London's Springfield Hospital to nurses on passing their final examinations (6). Livery survives in the modern uniforms worn by nurses, the police, the armed forces and others, but it is generally the badge that defines the individual's status.

3

4

5

6

1. *Cutlers' Company, UK, about 1772*
2. *Ascot Races, UK, 1938*
3. *British Museum, UK, probably about 1890*
4. *Air Raid Precaution, UK, 1939*
5. *Great Western Railway, UK, about 1940*
6. *Springfield Hospital, London, UK, about 1983*

membership

The sense of belonging that badges provide is most obviously conveyed by those issued by clubs and societies.

In the years between the wars many British newspapers set up children's clubs as a means of engaging younger readers. The *Daily Mirror*'s Wilfredian League of Gugnuncs (1) was established in 1927, and was named after the baby rabbit that appeared in the newspaper's Pip, Squeak and Wilfred cartoon strip and the baby-talk words 'gug' and 'nunc' that the character used. The League held meetings and parties and raised funds for children's charities. The Women's League of Health and Beauty, founded in 1930 to promote health exercise and dance for women, provided affordable fitness classes around the country. The design on its badges (2) is taken from a photograph of a leap performed by dancer and teacher Peggy St Lo. The Handicapped Childrens' Pilgrimage Trust was established in 1956 to organize pilgrimages to the Roman Catholic shrine of Lourdes; its badge was designed by wood-engraver Alan Taylor (3).

Badges of collectors' groups and historical societies generally include an appropriate historical image. An ancient Athenian drachm appears on a young coin collectors' badge issued by the publishers of *Coins, medals and currency* (4), whilst a badge of the Scottish Military Collectors Society bears a stylized Highland soldier designed by painter and illustrator Douglas Anderson (5). The figure on the exquisite gold badge of the Caryatids (a group of enthusiasts who provide the British Museum's Department of Greek and Roman Antiquities with advice and financial support) is the work of goldsmith Kevin Coates and is based on the upper portion of an ancient marble caryatid found near Rome and acquired by the British Museum from the collection of Charles Townley in 1805 (6).

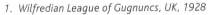

1. Wilfredian League of Gugnuncs, UK, 1928
2. Women's League of Health and Beauty, UK, about 1935
3. Handicapped Children's Pilgrimage Trust, UK, about 1960
4. Young Coin Collectors' Club, UK, 1969
5. Scottish Military Collectors Society, UK, about 1970
6. British Museum Caryatids, UK, 1990

advertisements

By the early twentieth century the badge was already widely used as an advertising tool. Functioning in a similar fashion to those proclaiming political beliefs, these badges encourage the wearer to identify with the product and also, in effect, turn that individual into a walking advertisement.

The organizers of the British Empire Exhibition, held in Wembley in north London in 1924, and the Festival of Britain, held in 1951, used badges with distinctive devices to promote these events. Both devices are updated versions of traditional patriotic themes: the British lion (1) and the head of Britannia (2). The latter is juxtaposed with a compass and celebratory bunting in national colours in a design by Abram Games. The first Butlin's holiday camp was opened in Skegness in 1936, and by the 1960s nearly a million people were staying in Butlin's camps each year. From the beginning attractive badges with individual designs for each camp and each year were issued, both to identify campers and to advertise the holidays (3).

The most influential marketing of a city through badges has been the 'I love New York' campaign, instituted in 1977 (4); the replacement of the word 'love' with a heart has subsequently been used around the world in countless contexts.

Badges are now routinely used by museums to advertise their temporary exhibitions, using objects from the exhibitions or images suggested by them (5-7); the Viking on the British Museum badge is by cartoonist Mel Calman. The wide range of commercial enterprises now issuing badges includes nightclubs (8), magazines (9) and television companies (10). The humorous *Marxism Today* badge places the comedian Groucho Marx alongside Karl Marx. The Granada television badge shows Castle Howard, the setting for an adaptation of Evelyn Waugh's 1945 novel, *Brideshead revisited*, first broadcast in 1981.

1

2

3

4

5

6

7

8

9

10

1. *British Empire Exhibition, UK, 1924*
2. *Festival of Britain, UK, 1951*
3. *Butlin's Holiday Camp, Clacton, UK, 1964*
4. *New York, USA, about 1980*
5. *'This brilliant year': Queen Victoria's jubilee 1887, Royal Academy, UK, 1977*

6. The Vikings, *British Museum, UK, 1980*
7. The art of the Van de Veldes, *National Maritime Museum, UK, 1982*
8. Mud Club, *UK, 1984*
9. Marxism Today, *UK, about 1986*
10. Brideshead revisited, *UK, about 1990*

art

The popularity of the badge – whether as a fashion statement, an outward projection of the inner self, or a means of communication – has led various well-known artists to explore the medium. Artists who have placed their art at the disposal of a political cause, such as Alexander Calder, are noted elsewhere in this book, as are the cartoonists Jules Feiffer, Ralph Steadman and Steve Bell. The cartoon has close parallels with the badge, for in both cases art is placed at the service of an idea and that idea is often most successfully expressed with an economy of means.

Other artists have participated in the creation of badges as works of art in their own right. In 1981 London's Angela Flowers Gallery issued twenty-five badges made up from original art works by contemporary artists. These included the painter Tom Phillips, whose two badges, one of which is shown here (1), relate to his book, *The Humument*, first published in 1976, a nineteenth-century text transformed into a new visual and verbal poetic statement through the artist's intervention. One of the two badges based on works by another painter, Patrick Hughes, uses two suns and a rainbow to recreate a 'smiley' face, a symbol of optimism and joy that first appeared in mid-1960s America; Hughes's other badge inverts the rainbow to produce a very different effect (2).

A badge issued by London's Goldsmiths' Company in 2000 to mark the passing of the millennium shows an engraved leopard taken from a silver bowl designed and made by goldsmith and jeweller Malcolm Appleby to mark the five-hundredth anniversary of the London Assay Office in 1978 (3). More recently, London-based sculptor and medallist Danuta Solowiej has turned to making her own badges that incorporate photographic images of her three-dimensional works – which thereby become more readily available (4).

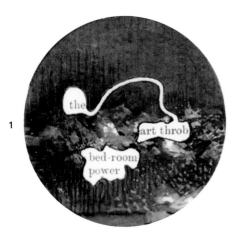

1. The art throb bed-room power *by Tom Phillips, UK, 1981*

2. Down in the mouth *by Patrick Hughes, UK, 1981*

3. Leopard *by Malcolm Appleby, UK, 2000*

4. Soulmates *by Danuta Solowiej, UK, 2002*

further reading

Philip Attwood, *Acquisitions of badges (1983-1987)*. *British Museum Occasional Paper 76* (London, 1990)
John Gorman, *Images of labour* (London, 1985)
Ted Hake, *The button book* (New York, 1972)
Paul Martin, *The trade union badge: material culture in action* (Aldershot, 2002)
Melissa Schrift, *Biography of a Chairman Mao badge: the creation and mass consumption of a personality cult* (New Brunswick, New Jersey, and London, 2001)

Michael Schröder (editor), *Button* (Berlin, 1982)
Ken Sequin, *The graphic art of the enamel badge* (London, 1999)
Frank R Setchfield, *The official badge collector's guide: from the 1890s to the 1980s* (Harlow, 1986)
Brian Spencer, *Pilgrim souvenirs and secular badges: medieval finds from excavations in London* (London, 1998)
Edmund B Sullivan, *Collecting political Americana* (New York, 1980)

donors

Amnesty International
Mr D N Anderson
Animus
Anti-Apartheid Movement
Miss M M Archibald
Mrs D H Attwood
Mr P Attwood
Mr E Baldwin
Mr C Binet
Dr R F Bland
Mrs V Bloomfield
Mr T R Blurton
Mr A E Brandon
Mr R M Butt
Ms A Calton
Campaign for Nuclear Disarmament
Mr J Carr
The Caryatids
Mr R J Clarke
Coalition for Peace through Security
Conservative Party
Dr B J Cook
Mr K Coombes
Mr S Coppel
Mrs G Courtney
Mr J E Cribb

Dr J E Curtis
Mr A J Daniels
Ms D Deamer
Ms D Delgado
Electric, Electronic, Telecommunications and Plumbing Union
Mr A J Ellis
Sir John Evans
Mr D Fearon
Prof R A Fischer through the British American Arts Association
Mr C Francis
Ms R Friedman
Dr J Fritz
Ms P Gaster
Mr V Graves
Mr C G Howson
Mr A Hughes
Professor and Mrs J Hull Grundy
Mr G T Innes
Mr N Jacobs
Mr M P Jones
Dr J P C Kent
Mr G Knights
Labour Party

Mr L A Lawrence
Mr M N Levin
Mr S Lytton
Ms J Maclean
The Hon Mrs Marten
Mr B T McCarthy
Mrs J B Mellor
Dr A Mikolajczyk
Mr J Mills
National Abortion Campaign
National and Local Government Officers' Association
National Union of the Footwear, Leather and Allied Trades
National Union of Public Employees
National Union of Railwaymen
Nicaragua Solidarity Campaign
Mr D Newrick
Organisationen til Oplysning om Atomkraft
Dr F Parkes Weber
Peace Pledge Union

Dr V A Porter
Mr G Poulton
Dr M J Price
Ms N Ramm
Miss M Randall
Mr E J Rapson
Mr R A Rush
Mr R Sandström
Ms F Simmons
Ms D Solowiej
Mr S Sparkes
Ms L Stagg
Dr H M Swiderská
Terrence Higgins Trust
Trades Unionists Against Section 28
Ulster Unionist Council
Mr G Way
Mr D Webb
Mr M Williams
Ms G Williamson
Ms C Wilmer
Miss D Wilson
Sir David Wilson
Mr T H Wilson
Mr R W Wright
Mr W Woodside
Ms S Yanowitz

illustration references

All the badges illustrated in this book are in the British Museum's Department of Coins and Medals, with the exception of those prefixed P&E below, which are in the Department of Prehistory and Europe. The numbers to the left indicate page numbers.

6	P&E 55,6-25,10		1988-6-24-6		1985-6-14-1		2003-5-63-1	80	1985-12-24-12
7	P&E 56, 7-1,2096		1985-9-38-21		1984-12-24-2		2003-5-7-14		1982-7-15-13
	P&E 2003,3-31,3		2003-5-56-2	47	1986-1-18-4	64	1988-2-3-3		1982-7-15-3
8	M7602	30	1906-11-3-3761		1987-12-57-11		1984-6-42-5	81	1985-6-25-1
9	M6135		1964-11-17-1		1987-12-7-7	65	1984-6-42-2		1990-10-20-15
	M6230	31	1984-7-11-3		1994-1-3-6		1986-5-33-5		1983-2-25-6
11	1998-4-22-20		1964-11-17-4	49	1984-5-1-1		1991-9-35-2		1989-5-24-6
13	1982-7-15-17		M8919		P&E1978,10-2,161	67	1978-7-5-202	82	1987-3-24-1
15	1987-4-22-2		1964-11-17-17	50	1995-10-9-3		1978-7-5-15		1990-12-6-6
	1987-2-3-5	33	1987-11-35-120		1987-11-35-629		1983-4-17-1	83	1994-6-6-4
	1985-7-77-4		1995-8-42-3		1997-1-38-4		1986-6-34-1		1993-5-37-2
	1985-4-13-10	34	1991-6-47-14	51	1978-7-5-65		1985-7-78-3		2003-5-60-1
	1984-10-24-1		1987-6-11-3		1986-1-28-2	68	1991-7-49-1	84	1989-2-8-5
	1984-11-10-1		1985-12-33-21		1985-12-33-3		1989-12-10-1		1989-2-8-7
	1983-1-25-1	35	1987-11-35-252	52	1906-11-3-688	69	1987-8-9-1		1986-6-37-1
16	M7291		1985-5-18-6		1906-11-3-687		1990-11-21-12		1985-12-42-1
	M6291		1994-6-9-9	53	1987-11-41-2		1988-4-9-12	85	1989-5-21-1
17	1906-11-3-698	36	1989-5-16-4		1906-11-3-681	70	1997-1-38-64		1996-8-39-4
	1985-5-35-7		M9003		1906-11-3-680		1997-1-37-23		2003-5-9-6
	1987-3-3-4		1978-7-5-170		1906-11-3-683		1982-7-15-2		2003-5-24-28
18	1985-6-40-1		1990-12-1-1	54	1987-1-29-1		1985-5-9-2	86	1893-2-2-1
	1990-12-8-45		1989-3-1-1		1990-12-8-90	71	1984-5-8-1		1998-4-21-19
	1984-4-2-1		1989-3-1-2		1984-7-32-6		1984-1-42-8	87	1933-3-9-1
19	1983-12-24-1	37	1994-4-22-1	55	1986-4-8-11		1985-4-13-6		1990-12-8-124
	1990-12-8-66		1995-8-20-1		1985-9-37-2		1990-12-4-1		1991-6-44-1
	1984-5-1-2		1998-4-15-9		1985-7-77-1		1994-2-19-1		1983-11-30-2
	1986-7-29-5	39	1987-3-26-1	57	1978-7-5-164	73	1985-2-16-1	89	2000-9-1-128
21	M5292	40	1978-7-5-183		1980-4-8-16		1987-11-35-515		1984-10-23-3
	M5287		1990-6-28-1		1978-7-5-256		1983-5-48-1		1978-12-18-3
	1906-11-3-474	41	1992-2-37-1		1983-3-25-1		1984-6-41-2		1985-11-38-10
23	M8934		1991-5-1-3		1983-11-2-9		1984-10-7-1		1986-8-9-3
24	1990-12-8-86	42	1990-12-10-2		1983-11-2-7		1987-12-10-49		1991-10-32-1
	1987-8-5-1		1990-12-10-5		1985-7-79-21		1988-6-24-2	91	1986-6-36-8
25	1987-8-5-4		1990-12-10-15		1987-4-12-1	74	1997-1-38-32		1987-2-8-1
	1990-12-8-94		1990-12-10-22		2003-5-31-1	75	1983-3-3-9		1986-1-27-55
	1987-1-30-1		1991-1-10-1	58	1986-1-28-4		1983-2-2-1		1986-7-36-146
	1987-1-30-2	43	1978-7-5-205		1987-11-35-499		1983-2-25-1		1986-7-36-27
26	1987-3-3-1		1990-6-9-3	59	1987-11-35-496		1983-12-24-3		1983-3-49-1
	1985-1-14-1		1992-7-5-3		1986-5-22-1		1988-8-19-1		1983-2-12-1
	1987-1-31-1	44	1983-12-14-545	60	1984-9-28-2		1988-2-3-1		1984-3-19-1
27	1987-4-23-2		1986-7-35-20		1984-11-15-3	76	1975-8-11-2		1986-7-4-4
	1987-12-57-12		1985-9-40-1	61	1984-11-15-1	77	1975-8-11-1		1991-9-16-3
	2003-5-17-5	45	1986-7-35-13		1985-9-37-13	78	1984-11-15-4	93	1982-8-9-21
29	1980-4-8-59		1985-7-13-1	62	1990-11-3-1		1987-4-2-5		1982-8-9-15
	1983-5-39-19		1985-7-34-1		1990-12-24-1	79	1988-4-9-4		2003-5-7-10
	1984-5-1-3		1985-7-34-2	63	1991-2-9-3		1978-7-5-19		2003-5-45-4
	1984-5-10-2		1985-7-34-3		1991-7-17-2		1990-10-20-31		
	1985-1-9-1	46	1983-4-32-2		1991-4-30-1		1982-12-10-1		

index